THiS BOOK BELONGS TO:

_____

STERN VIEW

decks

cannon

stern

port
side

starboard
side

general
stores

keel

stone
ballasts

rudder

galley stove

Amy Hevron

sunken ship

asts

sails

bow

anchor

hull

keel

SPANISH GALLEON

porthole

Beach Lane Books • New York London Toronto Sydney New Delhi

Long ago, a grand treasure ship journeyed across the Caribbean Sea.

One day, a storm swirled in.

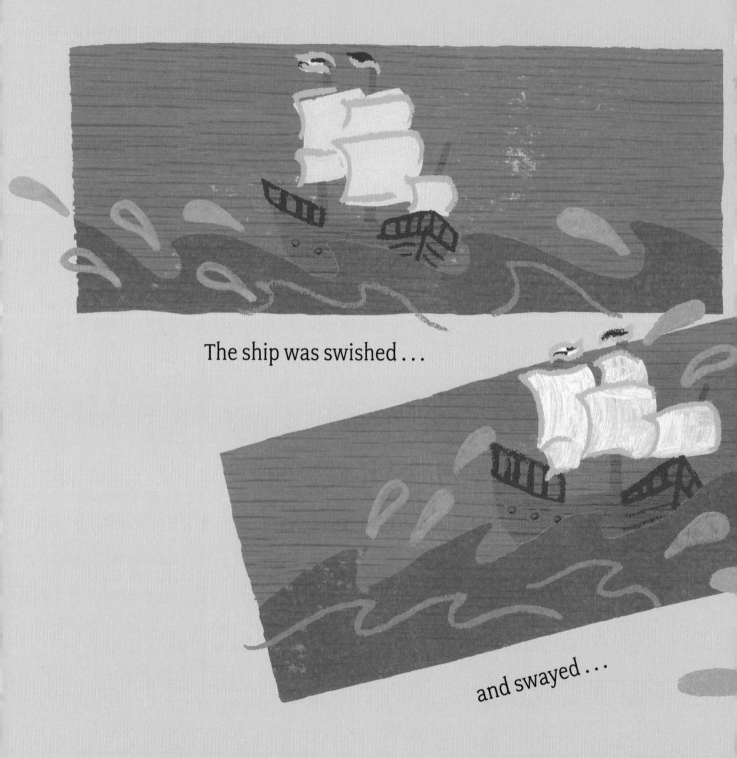

The ship was swished . . .

and swayed . . .

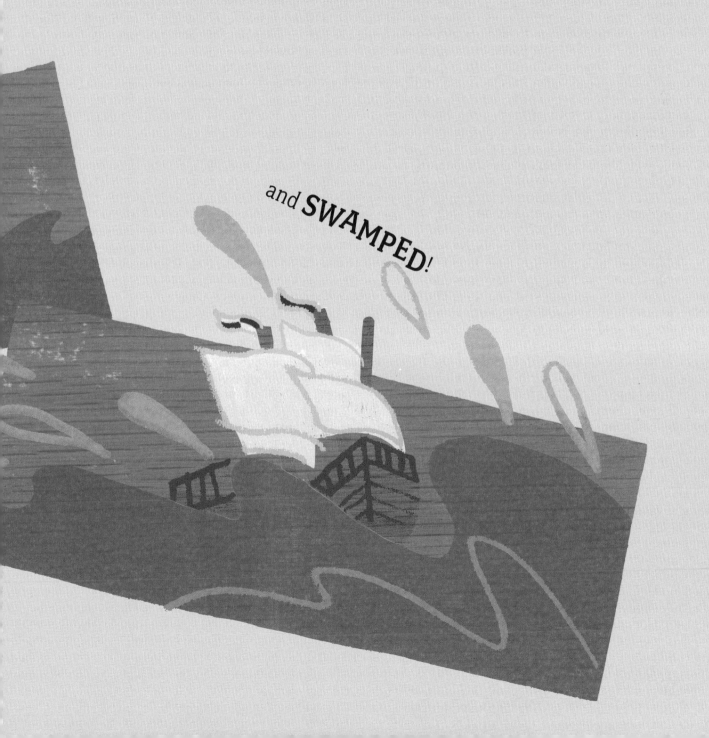

and SWAMPED!

As its crew swam to safety,
the ship sank down to the seabed.

There it would become a treasure ship
of a different kind.

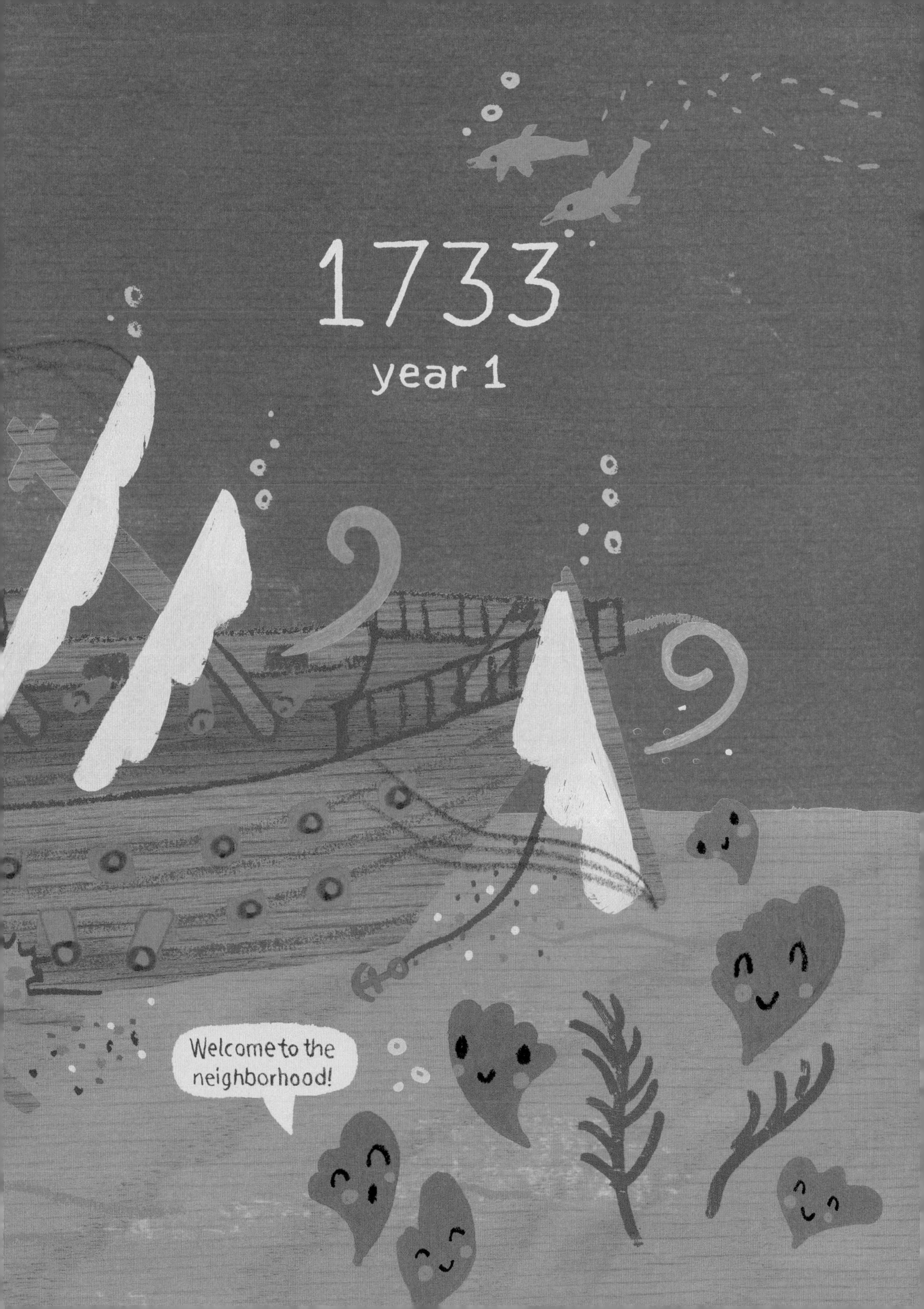
1733
year 1
Welcome to the neighborhood!

Algae and sea lettuce
were the first to move in.
They washed into the ship's
wooden hull.

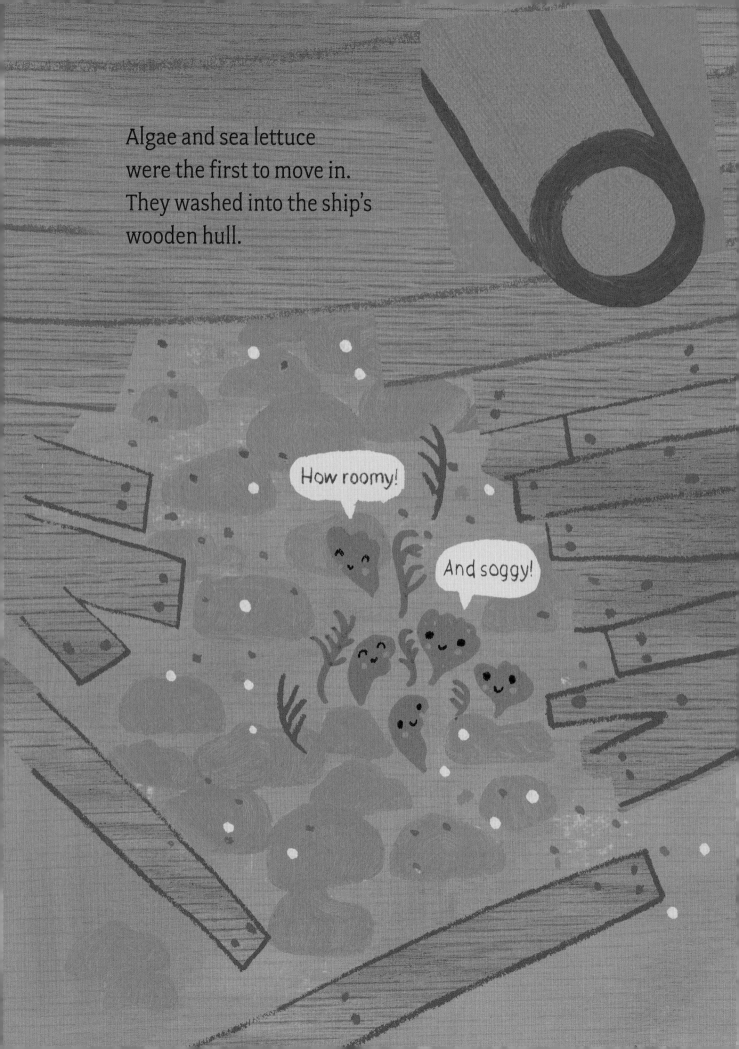

Soon, piddocks joined the crew.
They drilled into the damp deck.

Gribbles gobbled into
the mighty masts.

And schools of spadefish and butterfly
fish feasted on swirled-up plankton.

One night, after a full moon,
the currents carried in coral larvae.

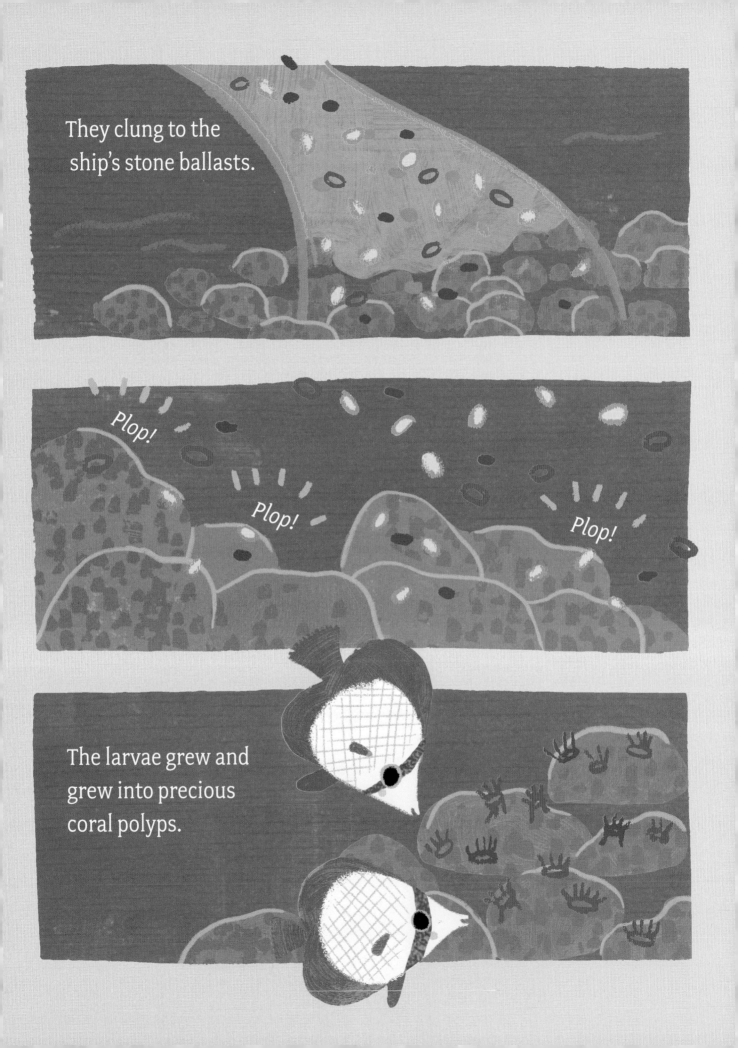

They clung to the
ship's stone ballasts.

Plop!

Plop!

Plop!

The larvae grew and
grew into precious
coral polyps.

Meanwhile, the ship settled into the sandy seabed.

Many moons passed overhead,
while below, the sunken ship became
an underwater nursery.

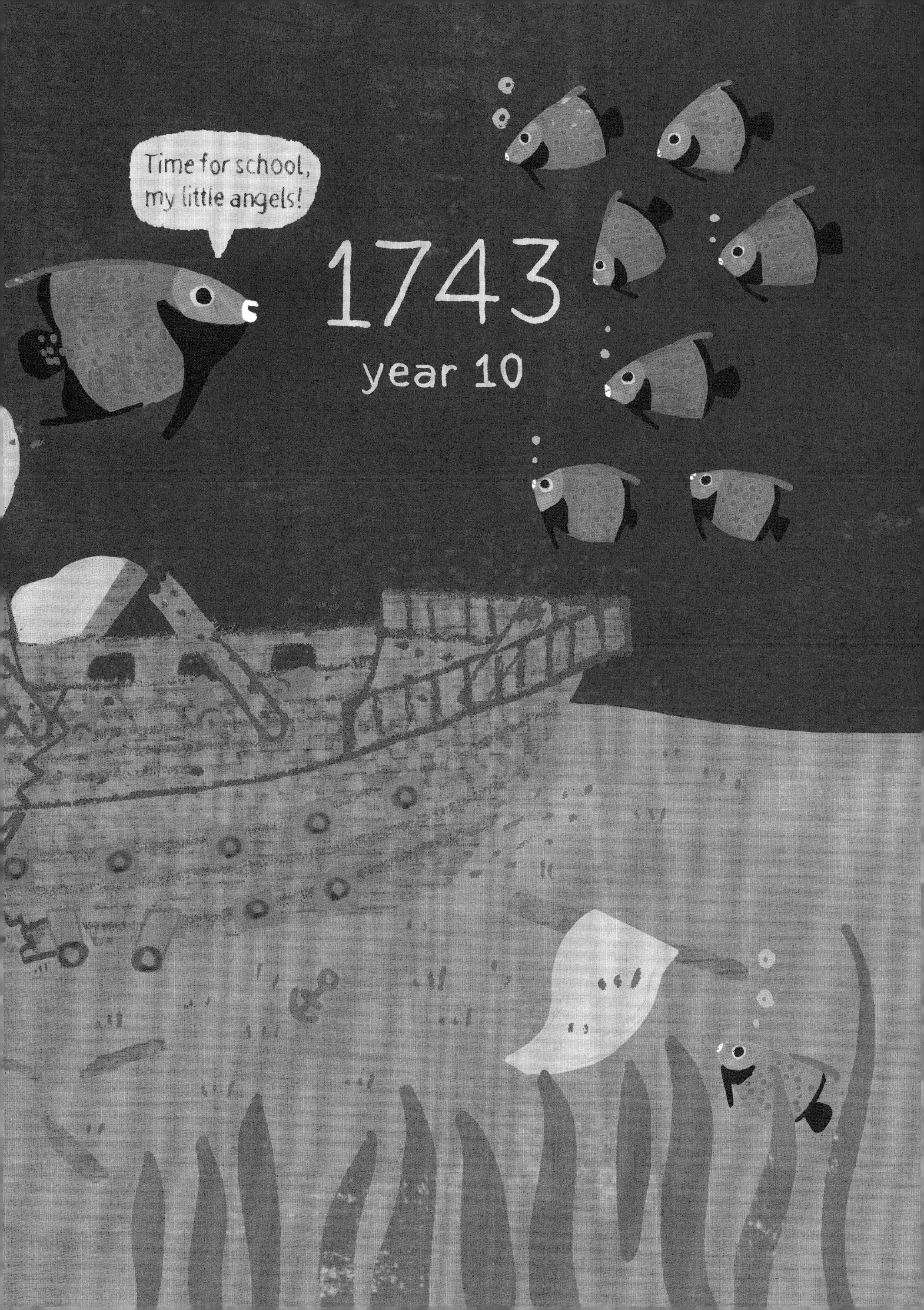
Time for school, my little angels!
1743
year 10

Baby blue tangs bobbed among its galley-stove bricks.

Good babies!
Eating all your algae!

Damselfish eggs sparkled on its starboard.

Twinkle!

Twinkle!

Little lobsters played
hide-and-seek on its port.

And the coral polyps budded into brilliant colonies of fire and starlet corals.

Meanwhile, the ship sank
deeper into the shifting sands.

As the years drifted by, more sea life flocked to the sanctuary of the sunken ship.

1833

year 100

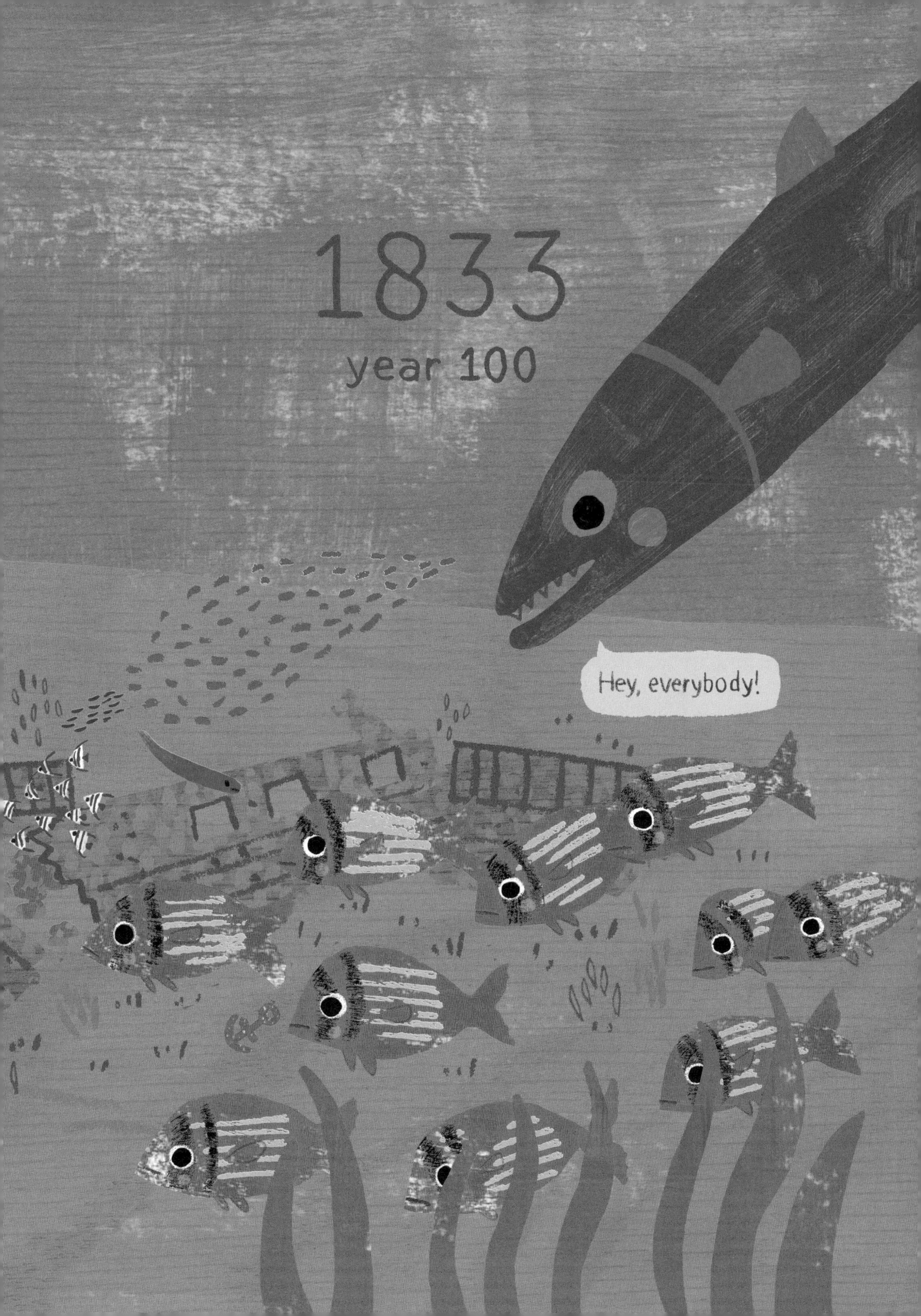

Crews of arrow crabs found food on its anemone-encrusted anchor.

Squads of reef squid found shelter
through its barnacle-laden portholes.

Lightning wrasses bolted into
its sponge-covered cannons.
And cannonball jellies boomed
above fields of seagrass.

Meanwhile, the ship
decomposed in the shifting sands.

Today, the remains of the sunken ship
are a rainbow of reef life.

present day

Bluestriped grunts stream
past a purple-mouthed moray eel.

Blimey! He's scary!

Yellow stingrays peek into pink vase sponges.

Where'd you
guys go?

Green sea turtles *snap, snap*

and flame scallops *clap, clap.*

Tee hee! So tickly!

The ship has become a
coral-reef treasure trove.

Now, when storms swirl in,
the schools of fish swish.

The sea fans sway.

The seagrasses sweep.

Let me know when the coast is clear!

Okay.

bottlenose dolphins

What a treasure!

And the sunken ship
is a safe harbor for all.

butterfly fish

parrotfish

barracuda

spiny lobster

lightning
wrasses

bluestriped grunts

queen conch

yellow stingray

flounder

nurse shark

cannonball jellyfish

damselfish

porkfish

sargeant majors

grouper

angelfish

reef squid

purplemouth
moray eel

sea turtle

adult
blue tang

arrow crabs

spadefish

juvenile
blue tang

More About Sunken-Ship Reefs

This story is inspired by the Spanish treasure ship the *San Pedro*, which sank off the coast of the Florida Keys during a hurricane in 1733. In the centuries that followed, it has become a rich reef ecosystem, home to a wealth of sea life, big and small. Sunken ships like the *San Pedro* and other human-made objects that become underwater reefs are referred to as artificial reefs. Sunken ships provide hard surfaces for coral polyps to cling to. They change seafloor currents to swirl up plankton, which attracts small fish, and then big fish. And over time, these artificial reefs become underwater oases, providing food and shelter to plants and animals in empty seafloor expanses.

Like natural coral reefs, artificial reefs can act as barriers to help mitigate coastline erosion and lessen ocean surges during hurricanes. And with natural reefs in distress around the world due to warming ocean temperatures, artificial reefs can help offset habitat loss for marine life. Researchers are continuing to study sunken-ship reefs to learn more about these fascinating ecosystems.

You can visit the *San Pedro* and other sunken-ship reefs in the Florida Keys National Marine Sanctuary. To learn more, check out https://floridakeys.noaa .gov/shipwrecktrail/welcome.html.

Additional Reading

Bissonette, Aimee M. *Shipwreck Reefs*. Park Ridge, Illinois: Albert Whitman & Co., 2021.

Gibbons, Gail. *Coral Reefs*, updated edition. New York: Holiday House, 2019.

Messner, Kate. *The Brilliant Deep: Rebuilding the World's Coral Reefs*. San Francisco: Chronicle Books, 2018.

Simon, Seymour. *Coral Reefs*. New York: HarperCollins, 2013.

Selected Sources

"1733 Spanish Galleon Trail." Florida Department of State, n.d. http://info.flheritage.com/galleon-trail/shipwreckpages/06_SanPedro.cfm.

"Experience the Treasures of the San Pedro." Florida State Parks, n.d. https://www.floridastateparks.org/learn/experience-treasures-san-pedro.

"Why Preserve Shipwrecks." National Park Service, September 28, 2017. https://www.nps.gov/articles/preserveshipwrecks.htm.

"There Are Artificial Reefs in Florida Keys National Marine Sanctuary." Florida National Marine Sanctuary/NOAA, n.d. https://floridakeys.noaa.gov/artificialreefs/arethere.html.

National Marine Sanctuaries/NOAA, n.d. https://sanctuaries.noaa.gov/science.

BEACH LANE BOOKS

An imprint of Simon & Schuster Children's Publishing Division • 1230 Avenue of the Americas, New York, New York 10020 • © 2024 by Amy Hevron • Book design by Lauren Rille • All rights reserved, including the right of reproduction in whole or in part in any form. • BEACH LANE BOOKS and colophon are trademarks of Simon & Schuster, LLC. • Simon & Schuster: Celebrating 100 Years of Publishing in 2024 • For information about special discounts for bulk purchases, please contact Simon & Schuster Special Sales at 1-866-506-1949 or business@simonandschuster.com. • The Simon & Schuster Speakers Bureau can bring authors to your live event. For more information or to book an event, contact the Simon & Schuster Speakers Bureau at 1-866-248-3049 or visit our website at www.simonspeakers.com. • The text for this book was set in Fairplex. • The illustrations for this book were rendered in acrylic, marker, and pencil on Bristol paper and digitally collaged. Manufactured in China • 0524 SCP

First Edition

10 9 8 7 6 5 4 3 2 1

Library of Congress Cataloging-in-Publication Data

Names: Hevron, Amy, author. • Title: Sunken ship / Amy Hevron. • Description: First edition. | New York : Beach Lane Books, [2024] | Series: Tiny habitats | Includes bibliographical references. | Audience: Ages 4–8 | Audience: Grades 2–3 | Summary: "Discover the tiny, fascinating world of underwater habitats on sunken ships that become artificial reefs"— Provided by publisher. • Identifiers: LCCN 2023049208 (print) | LCCN 2023049209 (ebook) | ISBN 9781665935005 (hardcover) | ISBN 9781665935012 (ebook) • Subjects: LCSH: Artificial reefs—Juvenile literature. | Ocean bottom ecology—Juvenile literature. | Marine habitats—Juvenile literature. | Shipwrecks—Juvenile literature. | Marine ecosystem health—Juvenile literature. • Classification: LCC QH541.5.O24 H48 2024 (print) | LCC QH541.5.O24 (ebook) | DDC 577.7/89—dc23/eng/20231213 • LC record available at https://lccn.loc.gov/2023049208 • LC ebook record available at https://lccn.loc.gov/2023049209